# WORKING FROM HOME WITH A CAT

## HEIDI MORENO

CHRONICLE BOOKS
SAN FRANCISCO

LIBRARY OF CONGRESS CATALOGING-IN-PUBLICATION DATA AVAILABLE.

ISBN 978-1-7972-0546-5

MANUFACTURED IN CHINA.

ILLUSTRATIONS BY HEIDI MORENO.
DESIGN BY HEIDI MORENO AND KIM DI SANTO.

10 9 8 7 6 5 4 3 2 1

CHRONICLE BOOKS LLC
680 SECOND STREET
SAN FRANCISCO, CA 94107
WWW.CHRONICLEBOOKS.COM

FOR DANNY, WHO HAS INSPIRED ME TO REACH FOR THE STARS. PEANUT AND I LOVE YOU MORE THAN ANYTHING.

# PACKAGES

WHERE DID I PLACE THE BRIEF PAPERS?!
I CANNOT BELIEVE I LOST THEM!!
WHAT IF I NEVER FIND THEM?!!
PROJECT BRIEF
VERY IMPORTANT
CONTRACT

LUNCH
TIME

INTERVIEW TIME

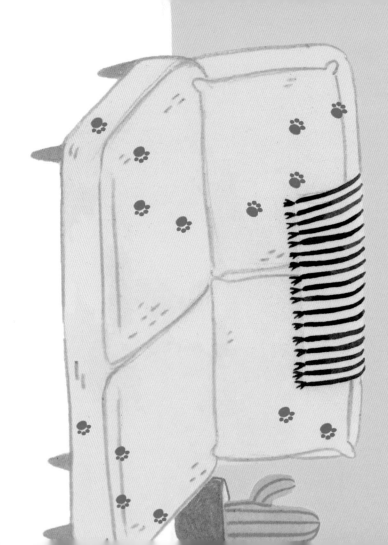

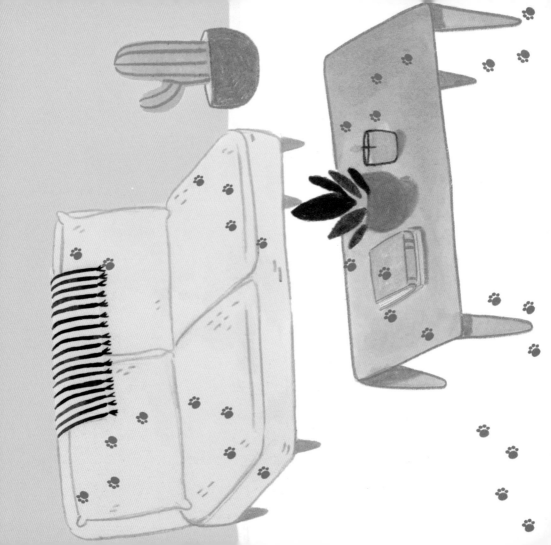

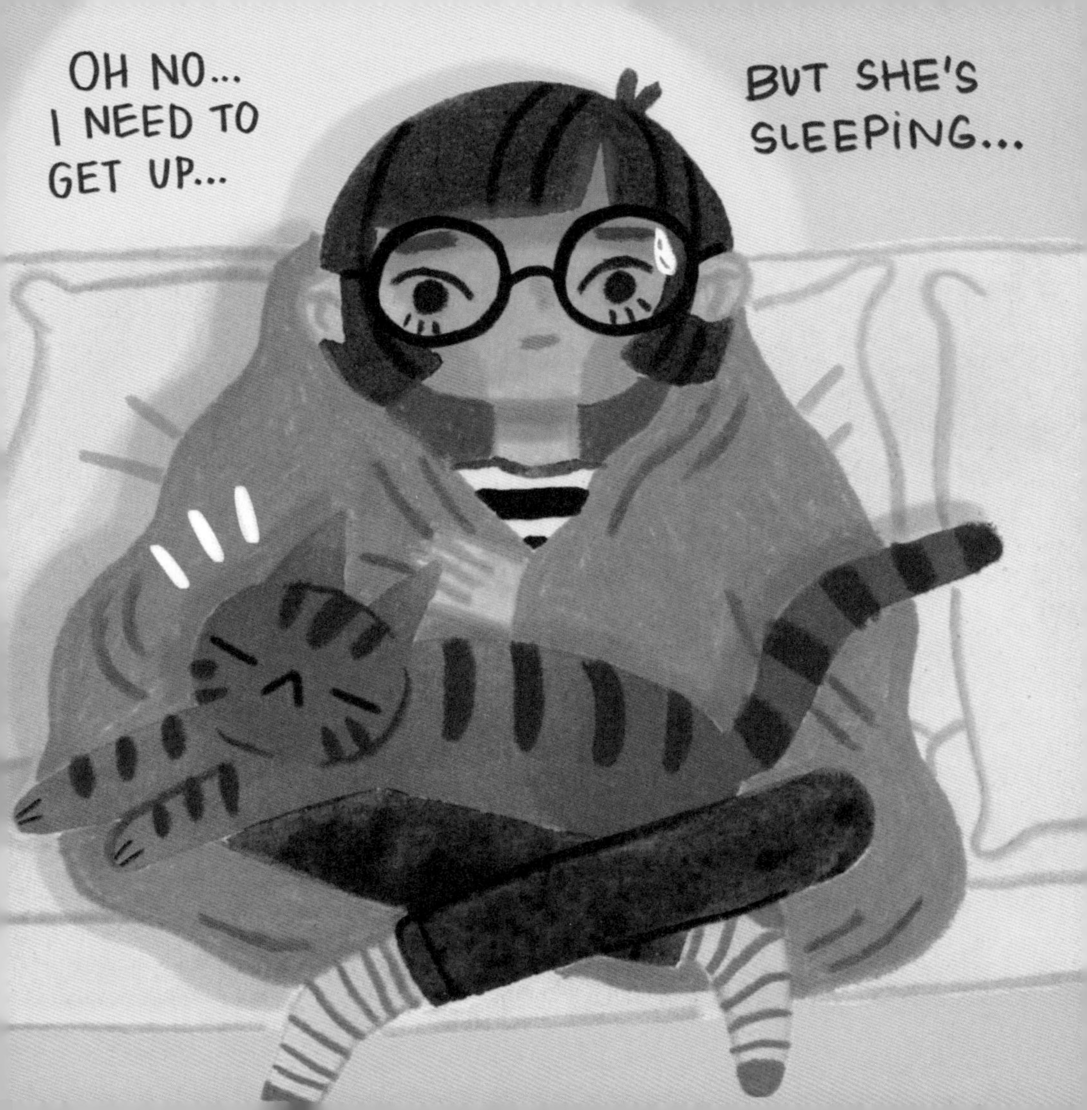
OH NO... I NEED TO GET UP...
BUT SHE'S SLEEPING...

# ABOUT THE AUTHOR

HEIDI MORENO IS AN ARTIST AND ILLUSTRATOR BASED IN THE LOS ANGELES AREA. SHE WORKS IN VARIOUS TRADITIONAL MEDIUMS LIKE WATERCOLOR, INK, AND COLORED PENCILS, AS WELL AS DIGITAL MEDIUMS. CATS HAVE ALWAYS BEEN A MAJOR SOURCE OF INSPIRATION GIVEN THEIR CUTE BUT SPOOKY AESTHETIC. SHE LIVES WITH HER CAT PEANUT AND HER SPACEMAN DANNY IN A SMALL HOUSE WITH A MASSIVE AVOCADO TREE IN THE BACKYARD.

PEANUT IS A TABBY CAT WITH A LOT OF PERSONALITY THAT SOMETIMES COMES ACROSS AS CATITTUDE. SHE PREFERS TRASH AND BUGS OVER ACTUAL CAT TOYS. MOST DAYS, YOU CAN FIND HER CATCHING LIZARDS IN THE BACKYARD OR UP TO SOME OTHER MISCHIEF.